AI Simplified

A Layman's Guide to
Understanding and
Utilizing Artificial
Intelligence

ZANE ARCHER

ISBN: 9798879975543

AI Simplified
A Layman's Guide to Understanding and Utilizing Artificial Intelligence

Copyright © 2024 by Zane Archer

To all who need to know and, perhaps,
overwhelmed by the information overload -
this book is for you.

This book is your friendly guide, ready to
demystify AI and make it understandable and
accessible.

AI for everyone!

**This guide cuts through the jargon,
so you can learn AI without feeling lost.**

Preface

Remember when robots were just bleep-blooping movie characters? Not anymore! AI is here, living rent-free in our phones, cars, and even our fridges! It's everywhere, shaping our world in ways both big and small.

But let's face it, AI can feel like a giant robot monster, confusing and scary. ✖ Fear not! This book is your friendly AI translator, here to banish the jargon and explain things in a way that makes even your grandma say, "Aha! I get it!"

Forget the dry tech talk and complicated algorithms. We'll break down AI into bite-sized pieces. So, whether you're a tech whiz kid or a curious retiree, this book is your ticket to understanding the amazing world of AI!

Table of Contents

What is AI, Really?

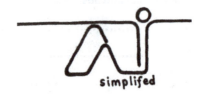

Unveiling the Mystery: From Science Fiction to Reality

We're embarking on a journey to demystify the concept that has long captured imaginations and fueled both curiosity and trepidation. AI, once relegated to the realms of science fiction, has become an integral part of our daily lives, shaping the way we work, communicate, and perceive the world.

AI is a vast and dynamic field, constantly pushing the boundaries of what machines can do.

Technically: AI refers to machines and software designed to imitate aspects of human intelligence. However, it's important to remember that AI systems don't truly "think" like humans. They operate on complex algorithms and statistical models, processing massive amounts of data to achieve their goals.

Functionally: AI exists in many forms, from simple rule-based systems to sophisticated deep learning models. Some familiar examples include:

- Recommender systems suggesting products you might like.

- Virtual assistants like Siri or Alexa responding to your voice commands.

- Self-driving cars navigating roads using sensors and AI algorithms.

- Spam filters automatically sorting your emails.

Philosophically: AI raises various questions about what it means to be intelligent, conscious, and truly alive. While we haven't reached "general intelligence" where machines can think and understand like humans across various domains, the rapid progress in AI sparks debates on ethics, potential risks, and the future of humanity's relationship with technology.

Impactfully: AI already significantly impacts our lives and is poised to play an even bigger role.

Understanding its various facets, from its technical underpinnings to its potential impact, is crucial for navigating the AI-driven world we live in.

Bridging the Imagination Gap

From the iconic HAL 9000 in "2001: A Space Odyssey" to the sentient machines in "The Matrix," science fiction has often depicted AI as either a benevolent ally or a malevolent force. However, the reality of AI is far more nuanced and multifaceted. In this chapter, we peel back the layers of speculation and delve into the historical foundations of Artificial Intelligence.

A Brief History: From Early Dreams to Modern Wonders

While the term "artificial intelligence" (AI) itself was coined in the mid-20th century, the seeds of the idea stretch back much further. Here's a whistle-stop tour through the key landmarks in AI's fascinating journey.

Ancient and Medieval Perspectives

Tales of automatons and thinking machines exist in ancient cultures worldwide, reflecting humanity's long-standing fascination with creating artificial intelligence. But even the ancients went farther than just dreaming about automatons.

Ancient Philosophical Thought

The Concept of Automata in Ancient Greek Philosophy

In the realm of ancient Greek philosophy, the concept of automata held a profound significance, reflecting the intellectual curiosity of thinkers such as Aristotle and other philosophers of antiquity. This exploration into the idea of automata provided an early foundation for the philosophical contemplation of artificial, self-moving entities.

Aristotle's Notions of Automated Action

Aristotle, one of the foremost philosophers of ancient Greece, delved into the concept of automata, primarily in his work "On the Soul" (Peri Psychēs). Within this treatise, Aristotle explored the nature of living beings and the principles underlying their actions. While his focus was primarily on the study of natural life, Aristotle's inquiries laid the groundwork for contemplating the possibility of artificial life.

The philosopher pondered whether it was conceivable to replicate such internal principles artificially, giving rise to the notion of artificial entities capable of autonomous action. While not explicitly discussing the creation of artificial beings, Aristotle's exploration of the underlying principles of life set the stage for later thinkers to contemplate the synthesis of living-like actions in non-biological forms — a concept that would echo through the centuries, influencing the development of automata and, eventually, artificial intelligence.

Mechanical Automata in Antiquity

The Antikythera Mechanism: A Greek Analog Computer

Within the realm of mechanical ingenuity in ancient Greece, the Antikythera Mechanism stands as a testament to early analog computing. Discovered in a shipwreck off the coast of the island of Antikythera, this intricate device dates back to the 2nd century BCE. Consisting of gears and mechanisms, the Antikythera Mechanism was designed to predict celestial movements, showcasing a level of technological sophistication that was not surpassed for centuries.

Water Clocks and Ancient Timekeeping Automata

In addition to celestial devices, ancient Greeks also experimented with water clocks as a means of automating timekeeping. These devices, such as the clepsydra, utilized the controlled flow of water to measure time intervals. The integration of automated mechanisms for timekeeping underscored the Greeks' early exploration of practical automata, laying the groundwork for later developments in clockwork technology.

Islamic Golden Age and Automaton Innovations

During the Islamic Golden Age, polymath Al-Jazari made significant contributions to the field of automata through his seminal work, "The Book of Knowledge of Ingenious Mechanical Devices." Composed in the 12th century, this treatise detailed the design and construction of various automated devices, including humanoid robots, musical automata, and sophisticated clocks. Al-Jazari's innovations reflected a fusion of engineering prowess and artistic creativity, marking a pinnacle in the medieval exploration of automaton technologies.

The Banu Musa Brothers and their Automaton Designs

The Banu Musa, three brothers of Persian descent, were influential figures in the medieval Islamic world. Their "Book of Ingenious Devices" outlined a myriad of automata, ranging from automatic doors to programmable machines. The brothers' emphasis on programmability hinted at an understanding of automated sequences, paving the way for future advancements in the field.

Medieval Alchemical Perspectives on Creating Artificial Life

In medieval Europe, alchemy played a central role in the conceptualization of creating artificial life. Alchemists, while primarily focused on transmuting base metals into gold and discovering the elixir of life, also delved into the notion of animating lifeless matter. The aspiration to mimic divine creation through alchemical processes provided a mystical foundation for later contemplations on artificial life.

Automata in Medieval European Cathedrals

The grandeur of medieval cathedrals went beyond religious symbolism; it extended to the incorporation of automata within these architectural marvels. Mechanical angels, clockwork animals, and other animated features adorned cathedrals, captivating the medieval audience with the fusion of spiritual and technological elements. These automata served both as religious allegories and marvels of engineering, showcasing the integration of mystical and mechanical perspectives.

Chinese and Indian Automata Traditions

The Han Dynasty's Mechanical Eunuch

In ancient China, the Han Dynasty witnessed the creation of a mechanical marvel – the "Dai Zai Qing Gong" or the mechanical eunuch. This humanoid automaton could perform complex movements, captivating audiences with its seemingly lifelike actions. The creation of such automata in ancient China demonstrated an early understanding of mechanics and articulated motion.

Indian Automata in Ancient Texts

Indian traditions also contributed to the exploration of automata, with ancient texts describing the use of mechanical devices for entertainment and religious rituals. These texts hinted at the existence of automaton traditions in ancient India, showcasing a diverse range of cultural perspectives on the creation and use of artificial entities.

Philosophical Implications for the Concept of Artificial Creation

The philosophical contemplations on artificial life and automata in ancient and medieval times laid the groundwork for profound questions about the nature of creation and existence. These early perspectives influenced not only technological advancements but also shaped the broader philosophical discourse on the boundaries between the natural and the artificial.

Philosophical Foundations

17th century: Rene Descartes and Gottfried Wilhelm Leibniz grappled with the nature of thinking and consciousness, laying the groundwork for symbolic reasoning and logic, essential aspects of early AI research.

The Dawn of the Machine Age

1940s: Development of the first programmable computers paves the way for practical applications of AI concepts.

Birth of AI (1950s-1970s)

1950: Alan Turing proposes the Turing Test as a benchmark for machine intelligence. In 1950, Alan Turing proposed the "Imitation Game," now famously known as the Turing Test, in his paper "Computing Machinery and Intelligence." The test involved a human judge interacting with both a human and a machine without knowing which was which. If the judge couldn't reliably distinguish between them based on their responses, the machine would be deemed intelligent. Turing's test not only laid the groundwork for discussions on machine intelligence but also delved into fundamental questions about consciousness, thought, and the nature of intelligence. The test sparked debates on the possibility of creating machines that could exhibit human-like behaviors, raising philosophical and ethical considerations that continue to resonate in contemporary AI discussions.

1956: The Dartmouth Workshop officially launches AI as an academic field.

1960s: Early successes in game playing (checkers, chess) and problem-solving fuel optimism.

1970s: Funding cuts and limitations of rule-based systems lead to an "AI Winter."

AI Revived (1980s-2000s)
1980s: Expert systems gain traction in specific domains like medical diagnosis.

1990s: Advancements in machine learning (ML) algorithms like neural networks lead to renewed interest.

2000s: Deep learning takes hold, enabling breakthroughs in speech recognition, image analysis, and other areas.

The Age of Deep Learning (2010s-present)
2010s: Continued progress in Deep Learning leads to powerful applications in healthcare, finance, transportation, and beyond.

2020s: Ethical considerations, explainability, and responsible development of AI become critical topics.

Early AI Programs and Languages

In the aftermath of the Dartmouth Conference, AI research gained momentum with the development of early AI programs and programming languages. The Logic Theorist, created by Allen Newell and Herbert A. Simon, and the General Problem Solver, by Newell and J.C. Shaw, stood as early milestones in AI, showcasing the potential for machines to solve complex problems.

AI Winters and Resurgences

However, the optimism of the early years was tempered by challenges, leading to periods known as "AI winters." Funding constraints and unmet expectations slowed progress. Yet, AI experienced resurgences, particularly with the advent of expert systems, which demonstrated the practical application of AI in specific domains.

Beyond the Buzzwords: Core Concepts of AI Explained

To truly understand AI, we must move beyond the buzzwords and catchphrases that often accompany discussions on the topic. Artificial intelligence is not a singular entity but a diverse and evolving field.

While "artificial intelligence" is often thrown around casually, understanding its core concepts requires diving deeper. Let's unpack some key terms:

1. **Machine Learning (ML):** This is the driving force behind much of today's AI advancements. It's where algorithms learn from data without explicit programming. Think of it as training a model to recognize patterns and make predictions based on new data. Popular ML approaches include:

  - **Supervised Learning:** The model learns from labeled data (e.g., cat pictures are labeled "cat").

o **Unsupervised Learning:** The model finds patterns in unlabeled data (e.g., grouping similar images without labels).

o **Reinforcement Learning:** The model learns through trial and error via rewards and penalties (e.g., teaching a robot to walk by rewarding successful steps).

2. **Deep Learning:** This is a specific type of ML inspired by the structure of the human brain. It uses artificial neural networks (ANNs) with interconnected layers to process information. Deep learning excels at complex tasks like image recognition and natural language processing (NLP).

3. **Natural Language Processing (NLP):** This subfield focuses on how computers understand and interact with human language. It allows machines to read text, translate languages, and even generate human-like text.

4. **Artificial General Intelligence (AGI):** This refers to hypothetical AI that can understand and learn any

intellectual task that a human can. We're still far from achieving AGI, and it raises significant philosophical and ethical concerns.

5. **Big Data:** This refers to the vast amount of data generated daily. ML algorithms need this data to learn and improve. However, ethical considerations regarding data privacy and bias are crucial.

6. **Robotics:** This field combines AI with mechanics to create intelligent machines that can move and interact with the physical world. Robots are increasingly used in manufacturing, healthcare, and even customer service.

AI is a vast and diverse field, and these are just some core concepts. Always look beyond the buzzwords and try to understand the underlying technology, it's application and most importantly, its implications.

AI in Your Pocket
(and Everywhere Else)

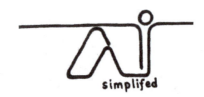

Artificial intelligence (AI) has quietly infiltrated our lives, weaving itself into the fabric of our daily routines. While we may not always recognize it, AI's invisible hand shapes our experiences in countless ways. Let's explore how AI is in your pocket and beyond.

Your Pocket AI

Smartphone: From facial recognition for unlocking to AI-powered assistants like Siri and Google Assistant, your phone is packed with AI features.

Social Media: AI algorithms curate your feed, personalize ads, and even suggest new connections.

17

E-commerce: Recommendation engines suggest products you might like, while fraud detection systems protect your financial information.

Beyond Your Pocket

Transportation: Ride-hailing apps use AI to optimize routes and predict demand, while self-driving cars inch closer to reality.

Healthcare: AI analyzes medical images, assists in diagnoses, and even powers chatbots for virtual consultations.

Finance: AI algorithms assess loan applications, manage investment portfolios, and combat financial fraud.

Entertainment: Streaming services recommend movies and shows based on your preferences, while AI-powered special effects bring fantastical worlds to life.

Manufacturing: Robots collaborate with humans on assembly lines, optimizing production and improving efficiency.

Climate Change: AI models predict weather patterns, assess environmental risks, and even optimize renewable energy usage.

The Invisible Force

Often, AI works behind the scenes, silently influencing our decisions and experiences. This invisibility can be both beneficial and concerning. Here are some key points to consider:

- **Convenience and Efficiency:** AI automates tasks, personalizes experiences, and optimizes processes, making our lives easier and more efficient.

- **Bias and Discrimination:** AI algorithms can perpetuate biases present in the data they're trained on, leading to discriminatory outcomes.

- **Privacy Concerns:** As AI collects and analyzes vast amounts of data, concerns about privacy and data security arise.

- **The Future of Work:** Automation through AI raises concerns about job displacement, necessitating workforce retraining and adaptation.

Understanding AI's role in our lives is crucial for shaping its future development responsibly. By demystifying the invisible force, we can harness its potential for good while mitigating its potential harms.

A Double-Edged Sword: Benefits and Concerns of AI

Artificial intelligence (AI) is rapidly transforming our world, offering immense potential for progress while also raising significant concerns. Just like a double-edged sword, it's crucial to understand both sides.

Benefits of AI
Innovation and Efficiency

AI excels at analyzing data, automating tasks, and optimizing processes. This leads to:

- Faster drug discovery and personalized medicine in healthcare.

- More efficient energy production and resource management for sustainability.

- Advanced robotics and automation in manufacturing, leading to greater production capacity.

- Enhanced transportation systems through self-driving cars and optimized traffic management.

Improved Decision-Making

AI can analyze vast amounts of data to provide insights and recommendations, improving decision-making in areas like:

- Financial analysis and risk prediction for businesses.

- Crime prevention and law enforcement by identifying patterns and predicting criminal activity.

- Education and personalized learning by tailoring education to individual student needs.

Concerns about AI
- **Job displacement:** Automation fueled by AI could lead to significant job losses in various sectors, requiring workforce retraining and adaptation.

- **Bias and discrimination:** AI algorithms trained on biased data can perpetuate societal inequalities and lead to discriminatory outcomes.

- **Privacy and data security:** Concerns exist about the vast amount of data collected and used by AI, raising privacy and security risks.

- **Weaponization and misuse:** The potential for AI-powered autonomous weapons poses significant ethical and security challenges.

- **Loss of control and autonomy:** Increased reliance on AI for decision-making raises concerns about human control and accountability.

Navigating the Future

Considering both the benefits and concerns, it's essential to approach AI development and deployment responsibly.

Transparency and accountability

AI systems should be explainable and auditable to ensure fairness and avoid bias.

Data privacy and security

Robust regulations and ethical practices are needed to protect personal data and ensure its responsible use.

Human-centered design

AI should be developed and used in ways that augment human capabilities and well-being rather than replacing them.

Public education and dialogue

Open discussions about AI's impact on society are crucial to foster trust and responsible development.

Ultimately, AI is a powerful tool with the potential to address major challenges and improve our lives. By acknowledging both its benefits and concerns, we can navigate its development and use responsibly, ensuring a future where AI serves humanity's best interests.

Unlocking the Magic: How Does AI Work?

Machine Learning Demystified: Algorithms & Data at Play

Algorithms are the linchpin of machine learning, acting as the guiding intelligence behind AI applications. Here, we dissect various types of algorithms, from classical approaches to cutting-edge deep learning models.

Data, the Fuel of AI

No discussion of machine learning is complete without acknowledging the critical role of data.

While "AI" often sounds complex and magical, it boils down to two key ingredients: algorithms and data. Let's delve into how these work together to power the machines learning around us:

The Learning Recipe

Imagine AI as a master chef following a special recipe. The algorithms are the recipe itself, outlining the steps the machine takes to process information and make decisions. The data is the diverse set of ingredients—text, images, numbers, etc.—that the AI uses to learn and improve.

Popular AI Recipes

Supervised Learning

Like following a detailed recipe with labelled ingredients (e.g., "cat" for cat pictures), the AI learns by comparing its predictions with known outcomes.

Unsupervised Learning

Imagine an adventurous chef experimenting with flavors (e.g., grouping similar images without labels). The AI finds patterns and relationships in unlabeled data.

Reinforcement Learning

Think of learning through trial and error like a chef receiving feedback ("too salty!"). The AI receives rewards for good results and learns to take better actions over time.

The Power of Data

Just like the quality of ingredients impacts a dish, the quality and quantity of data significantly affect AI performance. More data often leads to better outcomes, but ensuring diversity and representativeness is crucial to avoid biases in the AI's decisions.

Beyond the Recipe

While algorithms and data are essential, understanding AI fully requires considering other factors.

⇒ **Computational Power:** Complex algorithms need powerful computers to process large amounts of data efficiently.

⇒ **Human Expertise:** Data scientists and engineers design, train, and monitor AI systems, ensuring their functionality and addressing potential issues.

AI is not magic; it's a powerful tool that learns from data using specific algorithms.

Different "recipes" are better suited for different tasks, and the quality of data significantly impacts performance.

Human expertise remains crucial in guiding AI development and ensuring its responsible use.

Deep Learning Explained: Beyond Simple Rules

While traditional AI often relies on hand-crafted rules and logic, deep learning takes a different approach. Inspired by the structure and function of the human brain, it uses artificial neural networks (ANNs) to learn complex patterns from data.

Imagine a Brain in a Machine

Artificial neurons: These are the building blocks of ANNs, loosely mimicking real neurons. They receive inputs, process them, and send outputs to other neurons.

Layers: ANNs have multiple layers of interconnected neurons. Information flows from the input layer to the output layer, with each layer extracting more complex features.

Learning: Deep learning algorithms adjust the connections between neurons based on the data they see. This allows the network to learn and improve its ability to recognize patterns and make predictions.

Benefits of Going Deep

High accuracy: Deep learning excels at tasks like image recognition, speech recognition, and natural language processing, often exceeding human performance.

Adaptability: Deep learning models can learn from diverse data types and adapt to new situations without needing explicit reprogramming.

Scalability: They can handle massive datasets and complex problems, making them suitable for real-world applications.

Beyond the Hype

While powerful, deep learning isn't without its challenges.

Complexity

Designing and training deep learning models can be computationally expensive and require specialized expertise.

Data dependence

Deep learning models need large amounts of data to perform well, and biases in the data can lead to biased outcomes.

Explainability

Understanding how deep learning models arrive at their decisions can be difficult, raising concerns about transparency and accountability.

Natural Language Processing: Cracking the Code of Human Speech

Have you ever interacted with a chatbot, used voice commands on your phone, or translated text instantly online? These are all examples of Natural Language Processing (NLP) in action. This fascinating field helps computers understand and process human language, a seemingly simple task that's surprisingly complex.

The Challenge
Human language is nuanced and messy. We use slang, sarcasm, context, and implicit meanings that even the most advanced computers struggle to grasp. NLP tackles this challenge by employing various techniques.

Machine Learning
Algorithms are trained on massive amounts of text data to learn the patterns and rules of language.

Linguistics and NLP
Natural Language Processing (NLP) incorporates knowledge of grammar, syntax, and semantics to understand the structure and meaning of language.

NLP and Linguistics. The former, a potent force from computer science, equips machines with the ability to dissect and navigate the intricacies of human language. The latter, an established science rooted in human understanding, unravels the very fabric of how language works. Together, they form a symbiotic dance, each enriching the other's pursuit of comprehending the spoken and written word.

From Rules to Patterns

Traditionally, NLP relied on explicit linguistic rules, painstakingly encoded by experts. Yet, the sheer complexity and nuance of language often outmaneuvered these rigid structures. The tide turned with the advent of statistical and, more recently, deep learning approaches. NLP began mimicking the brain's ability to learn patterns from vast amounts of data, leading to a new era of adaptability and sophistication.

But even the most powerful algorithms still stumble in the face of ambiguity, sarcasm, and cultural references. This is where linguistics steps in, offering a treasure trove of knowledge about the structure, evolution, and social context of language. By shedding light on the subtle threads that connect words to meaning, linguistics empowers NLP to navigate the labyrinthine complexities of human expression.

This collaboration is not a one-way street. NLP's data-driven insights provide invaluable feedback to linguistic theories, challenging assumptions and revealing hidden patterns. For example, analyzing massive text corpora has exposed previously unknown grammatical structures and dialect variations, enriching our understanding of language evolution.

Statistical Analysis
Statistical models assess the probability of words appearing together, helping interpret meaning and intent.

Unlocking Potential
NLP enables computers to perform amazing tasks.

- Machine Translation: Breaking down language barriers by translating text and speech in real-time.

- Voice Assistants: Understanding spoken commands and responding in a natural way.

- Chatbots: Providing customer service and information in a conversational manner.

- Text Summarization: Condensing large amounts of text into key points.

- Sentiment Analysis: Understanding the emotional tone and opinion expressed in text.

Beyond the Headlines

NLP is not just about cool gadgets. It has real-world applications in various fields.

- **Healthcare**: Analyzing medical records to identify potential risks and improve diagnoses.

- **Finance**: Detecting fraud and analyzing financial documents.

- **Education**: Personalizing learning experiences based on individual needs.

> **Law**: Analyzing legal documents and predicting outcomes.

Looking Ahead

NLP is a rapidly evolving field with exciting possibilities.

o Natural Language Generation: Creating human-quality text for various purposes.

o Dialogue Systems: Engaging in open-ended, contextual conversations with humans.

o Multilingual Understanding: Processing and translating languages beyond standard translations.

The Challenges and the Promise

However, ethical considerations loom large. Biases embedded in data can perpetuate harmful stereotypes. The ability to manipulate language through NLP raises concerns about misinformation and propaganda. It is crucial to address these challenges with a collaborative spirit, ensuring that these powerful tools serve humanity's best interests.

As we delve deeper into the mysteries of language, the intertwined paths of NLP and Linguistics offer a glimmer of hope. By leveraging their combined strengths, we can not only bridge the gap between humans and machines but also forge a future where language becomes a tool for connection, understanding, and progress.

Responsible development and ethical considerations will be crucial in shaping the future of NLP and mitigating the realization of mankind's worst fears of this tool.

Quantum Computing and AI

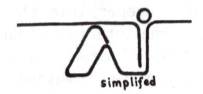

simplifed

First, What is a Quantum Computer?

Alright, let's imagine you have two kinds of super-smart helpers: classical computers (like the ones we use every day) and quantum computers (which are like magic computers).

Classical Computers:

Imagine you have a friend who loves solving puzzles. Every time you give them a puzzle, they look at all the possibilities and pick the best answer. This is how our regular computers work—they look at each option, one after the other, and choose the best one. It's like going through a list of toys and picking your favorite.

Quantum Computers:

Now, imagine you have a magical friend named Quantum. Quantum can do something incredible called "superposition." It's like having a magical toy that can be in two places at once! Instead of looking at each toy one by one, Quantum can look at all the toys at the same time and pick the best one. It's as if Quantum is super fast and super smart because of this magical ability.

Quantum can also do another trick called "entanglement." Let's say you have two magical toys, and when you touch one, the other one reacts, no matter how far apart they are. It's like having a twin toy that always knows what the other is doing. This makes Quantum really special because it can share information super quickly.

Putting it Together

Now, imagine you have a super big puzzle with lots and lots of possibilities. Your regular friend (classical computer) would take a long time to figure out the best solution because they check one possibility at a time. But Quantum, with its superposition and entanglement tricks, can check many possibilities at once and find the answer much faster!

So, when people talk about using Quantum computers for artificial intelligence (AI), they mean using these magical computers to solve really tricky problems way faster than our regular computers can. It's like having a super-speedy, super-smart friend who can help us with the most challenging puzzles in the world!

In the realm of computing, a paradigm shift is underway with the integration of quantum computing into the landscape of artificial intelligence (AI). Understanding this synergy requires a grasp of the unique principles governing quantum mechanics and the transformative potential it holds for AI applications.

Quantum Computing Fundamentals

At the heart of quantum computing lies the principle of superposition. In classical computing, information is processed using bits, each representing either a 0 or a 1. Quantum bits, or qubits, possess a remarkable property —

they can exist in multiple states simultaneously, thanks to superposition. This allows quantum computers to explore numerous possibilities at once.

Entanglement further elevates the capabilities of quantum computing. When qubits become entangled, the state of one qubit becomes directly linked to the state of another, regardless of the physical distance between them. This instantaneous correlation facilitates rapid information transfer and processing.

Quantum Computers and AI: Unleashing Parallelism

The advantage of quantum computing in the realm of AI becomes apparent when dealing with complex problems that involve sifting through myriad possibilities. Classical computers, operating sequentially, assess each option one at a time. Quantum computers, leveraging superposition, can evaluate multiple possibilities concurrently, exponentially enhancing computational speed.

Quantum Machine Learning and Algorithmic Advancements

The integration of quantum mechanics with AI extends to quantum machine learning algorithms. These algorithms harness the unique capabilities of quantum computers to perform specific tasks more efficiently than their classical counterparts. Quantum support vector machines and quantum neural networks exemplify this convergence, showcasing the potential for quantum computing to redefine the landscape of machine learning.

Challenges and Solutions: Quantum Decoherence and Integration

While the promises of quantum computing are immense, challenges must be addressed for practical implementation. Quantum decoherence, the susceptibility of quantum states to environmental interference, poses a significant hurdle. Efforts in quantum error correction are underway to mitigate this challenge, ensuring the stability and reliability of quantum computations.

Moreover, integrating quantum and classical systems presents complexities. Quantum computing operates on fundamentally different principles than classical computing. But breaking those boundaries is what humanity's advancement is all about.

Shared Intersection

- **Quantum-inspired AI:** Techniques from quantum computing can be used to develop new AI algorithms, potentially improving efficiency and tackling complex problems faster.

- **AI for Quantum Computing:** AI can help manage and optimize quantum computers, making them more user-friendly and accessible.

- **Shared Challenges:** Both fields face challenges like explainability, fairness, and security, requiring careful development and ethical considerations.

Real-world Applications: Quantum-enhanced Optimization and Machine Learning

Concrete applications of quantum computing in AI are emerging. Quantum-enhanced optimization, with its ability to explore vast solution spaces simultaneously, holds promise for industries grappling with complex decision-making processes.

Ethical Considerations: Quantum Security and Responsible Development

The convergence of quantum computing and AI prompts ethical considerations. Quantum computing's potential to break classical encryption methods raises questions about data security. Responsible development practices, ethical AI considerations, and societal impacts underscore the need for a thoughtful approach to the integration of these cutting-edge technologies.

Friend or Foe?

The rise of AI brings immense potential, but also raises ethical concerns that demand careful consideration. Let's delve into three key areas:

Privacy Concerns: Protecting Your Personal Data:

AI thrives on data, often personal data collected from various sources. This raises concerns about:

- **Transparency**: What data is collected and how is it used?

- **Consent**: Who gives consent and is it truly informed and freely given?

- **Security**: How secure is the data from breaches and misuse?

Solutions

◎ **Stronger data privacy regulations**: Enacting stricter laws like GDPR to empower individuals and ensure responsible data collection and use.

◎ **Privacy-preserving AI techniques**: Developing methods that allow AI to learn without compromising personal data.

◎ **Individual awareness and control**: Providing users with clear information and tools to manage their data privacy.

Job Displacement: Adapting to a Changing World

❷ **Automation**: AI automates tasks, potentially leading to job losses in some sectors.

❷ **Economic Impact**: Will job losses outweigh job creation from AI-driven industries?

- **Social Impact:** How will displaced workers transition to new jobs?

Solutions

- Reskilling and upskilling programs: Equipping workers with skills relevant to the AI-driven economy.

- Universal basic income (UBI): Providing financial security during transitions and fostering innovation.

- Ethical guidelines for AI development: Ensuring AI development considers human well-being and minimizes job displacement.

Beyond Privacy and Jobs: A Broader Ethical Lens

Algorithmic Bias and discrimination

AI algorithms can perpetuate biases present in the data they're trained on, leading to discriminatory outcomes.

As AI infiltrates more aspects of our lives, the specter of algorithmic bias looms large. This bias arises when algorithms unintentionally discriminate against certain groups of people, perpetuating existing societal inequalities.

Understanding the Bias

Data-driven bias

Algorithms learn from data, and if that data reflects existing biases, the AI inherits them. For example, an algorithm trained on biased hiring data might unfairly favor certain resumes.

Algorithmic design

Inherent assumptions and choices made during algorithm development can unintentionally lead to biased outcomes. For instance, facial recognition systems trained primarily on white faces might struggle to accurately identify faces of other races.

Impacts of Bias

- **Unequal opportunities:** Biased algorithms can unfairly disadvantage individuals in areas like loan approvals, criminal justice, and healthcare access.

- ❷ **Erosion of trust:** When people perceive AI as biased, it can lead to distrust and resistance towards its adoption.

- ❷ **Widening the inequality gap:** Biased AI can exacerbate existing societal inequalities, further marginalizing vulnerable communities.

Combating Bias

◎⁝ Data auditing and cleaning

Identifying and mitigating biases present in training data is crucial.

◎⁝ Diversity and inclusion in AI teams

Enlisting diverse perspectives during algorithm development helps identify and challenge potential biases.

◎⁝ Explainable AI (XAI)

Developing AI systems that explain their decisions helps identify and address potential biases.

◎ Continuous monitoring and evaluation

Regularly assessing AI systems for fairness and mitigating emerging biases is vital.

Weaponization of AI

The potential for autonomous weapons raises serious ethical and safety concerns.

AI already plays keys roles in defense and security. From autonomous drones and intelligent surveillance systems to predictive analytics for strategic decision-making, the integration of AI in military applications is transforming the nature of warfare and security operations.

Ethical Dilemmas

The weaponization of AI brings forth a myriad of ethical challenges. Thus, we are inevitably confronted with the moral quandaries surrounding the use of autonomous weapons, the potential for indiscriminate targeting, and the blurred lines between combatants and civilians.

Transparency and explainability

Understanding how AI decisions are made is crucial for accountability and trust. **Transparency** and **Explainability** (XAI) are crucial aspects of developing trustworthy and ethical AI systems. They involve understanding how and why AI models make decisions, fostering trust, and mitigating potential risks. Here's a breakdown:

XAI: What is it?

Transparency

Openness about the design, data, and operation of AI systems. It involves disclosing information like:

⇒ How the system was developed and trained

⇒ What data it was trained on

⇒ How it makes decisions

⇒ Who is responsible for its development and deployment.

Explainability

The ability to understand the rationale behind an AI system's decision in a human-interpretable way. This can involve:

⇒ Explaining why a specific prediction was made

⇒ Identifying the most important factors influencing the decision

⇒ Highlighting potential biases or limitations of the system

Why is it important?

- **Building trust:** When people understand how AI systems work, they are more likely to trust their decisions and outcomes.

- **Accountability:** Transparency is essential for holding developers and users accountable for the actions of AI systems.

- **Avoiding bias:** Explainability helps identify and mitigate potential biases in the data or algorithms used to train AI systems.

- **Debugging and improvement:** Understanding how AI systems work is crucial for debugging errors and improving their performance.

Building Responsible AI

Global governance and cooperation

Addressing the ethical implications of AI requires international collaboration and responsible development principles. Implementing regulations that promote responsible AI development and protect individuals from discriminatory outcomes is necessary.

AI is not inherently good or bad; its impact depends on how we develop and use it. By fostering open dialogue, exploring solutions, and prioritizing ethical considerations, we can shape AI as a force for good in our world.

Establishing ethical principles for AI development helps ensure fairness, transparency, and accountability.

Open discussions about the potential impact of AI and its biases are crucial for responsible development.

Human-in-the-Loop

Human-in-the-Loop (HITL) paradigm stands as a transformative approach that converges the capabilities of artificial intelligence with the unique strengths of human intelligence. This collaborative dynamic goes beyond conventional narratives of fully autonomous AI, recognizing the inherent value of human intuition, ethics, and contextual understanding in decision-making processes.

The Fundamental Principles of HITL Dynamics

At its core, the Human-in-the-Loop paradigm emphasizes a symbiotic relationship between AI systems and human intelligence. Unlike scenarios where AI operates in isolation, HITL involves humans actively participating in the decision-making loop. This fundamental shift encourages a holistic perspective, where AI serves as a powerful tool for data processing, pattern recognition, and analysis, while humans contribute their nuanced understanding, ethical considerations, and contextual insights.

AI as an Augmentation Tool: Enhancing Human Decision-Making

HITL leverages AI as an augmentation tool, enhancing human decision-making across various domains. By processing vast datasets, identifying intricate patterns, and providing valuable insights, AI assists individuals in making more informed and efficient decisions. This collaborative approach is particularly evident in fields such as healthcare, where AI aids in medical diagnoses, and finance, where it supports risk management, illustrating how HITL can empower professionals in diverse industries.

Balancing AI systems to work collaboratively with human oversight mechanisms, leverages human judgment for critical decisions.

Shaping the Future with AI

While acknowledging the challenges and ethical concerns surrounding AI, it's also important to recognize its immense potential to address pressing global issues and create a better future for all. Let's explore some exciting areas where AI is making a positive impact:

1. Climate Change

> Optimizing renewable energy production and distribution.

> Monitoring environmental changes and predicting weather patterns.

> Developing sustainable agricultural practices and reducing food waste.

> Designing sustainable cities and infrastructure.

2. Healthcare

> Personalizing medicine and treatment based on individual needs.

> Early detection and diagnosis of diseases.

> Developing new drugs and therapies.

> Assisting doctors and nurses in providing care.

3. Education

> Adapting learning experiences to individual student needs and pace.

> Providing personalized tutoring and support.

> Making educational resources more accessible globally.

> Developing AI-powered language learning tools.

4. Global Development
> Improving agricultural yields and food security in impoverished regions.

> Predicting and managing natural disasters.

> Providing access to information and communication technologies.

> Combating poverty and inequality.

5. Sustainability and Resource Management
> Optimizing resource utilization and reducing waste.

> Preserving biodiversity and protecting ecosystems.

> Developing sustainable energy solutions.

➤ Monitoring and managing pollution levels.

Beyond these specific areas, AI can also contribute to:

⇒ Promoting peace and security by resolving conflicts and predicting violence.

⇒ Ensuring access to clean water and sanitation.

⇒ Strengthening democratic processes and citizen participation.

⇒ Empowering individuals and communities.

Harnessing the potential of AI for good requires.

1. Responsible development and ethical considerations.

2. Collaboration between diverse stakeholders (scientists, policymakers, communities).

3. Public awareness and education about AI's potential and limitations.

Investing in research and development for socially beneficial AI applications.
By proactively shaping AI's development and ensuring its responsible use, we can unlock its vast potential to address global challenges and create a more sustainable, equitable, and prosperous future for all.

Building a Responsible AI Ecosystem
Building a responsible AI ecosystem is critical to ensure AI development and deployment benefit everyone. This involves multiple crucial aspects:

1. Ethical Principles and Frameworks

⇒ Establish clear ethical guidelines and frameworks like the Montreal Declaration for Responsible AI.

These principles should focus on transparency, accountability, fairness, non-discrimination, and human well-being.

⇒ Promote public engagement and dialogue about AI's ethical implications and encourage diverse perspectives in design and development.

2. Data Governance and Privacy

⇒ Implement robust data privacy regulations like GDPR and CCPA that empower individuals and prevent misuse of personal data.

⇒ Develop and utilize privacy-preserving AI techniques like federated learning and differential privacy to protect sensitive information while enabling AI advancement.

⇒ Promote data openness and access while ensuring responsible data sharing practices and addressing data ownership complexities.

3. Bias Mitigation and Fairness

⇒ Audit and clean training data to identify and mitigate biases that can lead to discriminatory outcomes.

⇒ Develop diverse and inclusive AI teams to challenge biases and ensure different perspectives are considered during development.

⇒ Implement explainable AI (XAI) methods that make AI decisions transparent and understandable, enabling bias detection and correction.

4. Governance and Oversight

⇒ Establish clear regulatory frameworks for AI that balance innovation with responsible development and risk mitigation.

⇒ Promote international collaboration on AI governance to address global challenges and ensure responsible development across borders.

⇒ Empower oversight bodies to monitor AI development and deployment, investigate potential harms, and enforce ethical guidelines.

5. Education and Workforce Development

⇒ Increase public awareness and understanding of AI capabilities, limitations, and potential impacts.

⇒ Equip individuals with the skills needed to thrive in an AI-driven world, including digital literacy, critical thinking, and adaptability.

⇒ Upskill and reskill workers potentially displaced by automation to ensure a smooth transition to new opportunities.

6. Social Responsibility and Sustainability

⇒ Prioritize using AI for social good in areas like healthcare, education, climate change, and sustainability.

⇒ Develop AI applications that are inclusive and contribute to a more equitable society.

⇒ Consider the environmental impact of AI development and operation, promoting energy efficiency and sustainable practices.

By actively participating in the conversation, holding developers and policymakers accountable, and advocating for ethical principles, we can ensure AI serves humanity's best interests and shapes a brighter future for all.

You and AI

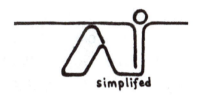

simplifed

As we conclude this exploration of AI, it's crucial to remember that we, not machines, ultimately hold the reins of the future. AI is a powerful tool, but like any tool, its impact depends on how we choose to use it. This is where you, an individual with unique perspectives and values, come in.

From the anticipatory nature of smart assistants to the tailored content suggestions from recommendation algorithms, AI establishes itself as a responsive companion, customizing experiences based on your unique preferences, behaviors, and needs. The realm of personalized interactions transcends mere convenience, creating a symbiotic relationship that adapts and evolves with your individual patterns.

Beyond streamlining tasks, AI empowers you in decision-making processes. Whether it's personalized financial insights or health-related recommendations, AI serves as a valuable information source, enabling you to make more informed choices. The transformative potential of AI lies not only in its convenience but in its contribution to your personal growth and well-being.

Key takeaways
Understand AI: The more you know about AI capabilities, limitations, and potential impacts, the more empowered you are to engage in informed discussions and shape its development.

Be critically aware: Don't blindly accept everything AI presents. Question its decisions, understand its biases, and advocate for fairness and transparency.

Demand responsible AI: Support organizations and initiatives that promote ethical AI development and hold developers and policymakers accountable.

Get involved: Share your voice, participate in discussions, and contribute to shaping the future of AI that aligns with your values.

Embrace the positive: Recognize the potential of AI to address global challenges, improve lives, and create a better future. Don't let fear or negativity hinder its responsible development.

AI is not a distant force threatening our existence. It's a tool in our hands, and we have the power to shape it into a force for good. By working together, actively participating, and demanding responsible development, we can ensure AI serves humanity's best interests and creates a future where humans and AI coexist and collaborate for a brighter tomorrow.

Summarizing AI Milestones

From ancient philosophical musings on automata to the groundbreaking work of Alan Turing and the formal birth of AI at the Dartmouth Conference, the development of AI has been a journey marked by theoretical insights, technological breakthroughs, and societal implications, laying the foundation for the intelligent systems we interact with today.

The field has weathered AI winters and celebrated resurgences, navigated the intricacies of symbolic reasoning and embraced the power of machine learning. The interplay between theory and application, philosophy and engineering, has defined AI's dynamic character.

Looking Towards the Future
As we peer into the future, the horizon of AI appears both promising and challenging. Quantum computing introduces a new dimension, offering unprecedented computational power with potential implications for AI. Ethical considerations, responsible development practices, and the societal impact of intelligent systems demand our attention. The quest for artificial general intelligence (AGI) continues, accompanied by ongoing debates about the ethical use of AI and the need for transparency and accountability.

The fusion of AI with other emerging technologies, such as quantum computing, augmented reality, and decentralized systems, presents exciting possibilities.

Importantly, the integration of explainable AI, robust ethical frameworks, and interdisciplinary collaboration will be pivotal in ensuring that AI development aligns with human values and societal well-being.

This is just the beginning of the conversation. Keep learning, keep questioning, and keep shaping the future with AI.

www.ingramcontent.com/pod-product-compliance
Lightning Source LLC
Chambersburg PA
CBHW071552080326
40690CB00056B/1809